THE ZACK FILES™

Dr. Jekyll, Orthodontist

THE ZACK FILES™

Dr. Jekyll, Orthodontist

by Dan Greenburg
Illustrated by Jack E. Davis

This Korean and English edition was published by Longtail Books, Inc. in 2020 by arrangement with Sheldon Fogelman Agency, Inc. through KCC(Korea Copyright Center Inc.), Seoul.

ISBN 979-11-86701-58-4 14740

Longtail Books

I'd like to thank my editors,
Jane O'Connor and Judy Donnelly,
who make the process of writing and revising
so much fun, and without whom
these books would not exist.

I also want to thank
Jennifer Dussling and Laura Driscoll
for their terrific ideas.

For Judith, and for the real Zack,
with love—D.G.

Chapter 1

My name is Zack. I'm a pretty normal kid. But **weird** things happen to me all the time. If a weird thing has a choice of happening to me or to somebody else, it always picks me. I don't know why.

Like one time a ghost named Wanda **trash**ed our apartment. Another time I got an **electric** shock in science class and for a while I could read everybody's mind. Also, about the best way to get to the **parallel universe**[1] next to ours is through the **medicine cabinet** in my bathroom.

Well, you get the idea.

Anyway, you might not think that going to an orthodontist[2] would lead to a weird and **scary adventure**. But you'd be wrong.

The time I want to tell you about started out normal enough. I went to the orthodontist because I had to have a baby tooth[3] pulled.

---

1 **parallel universe** 평행 우주. 공상 과학 소설이나 영화 등에서 사용하는 표현으로, 자신이 살고 있는 세계가 아닌 평행선 상에 위치한 또 다른 세계를 가리킨다.

2 **orthodontist** 교정 전문의. 비뚤어지거나 어긋난 치아 배열을 바르게 하는 교정 치료를 전문으로 하는 치과 의사.

3 **baby tooth** 유치 또는 젖니. 유아기 때 사용하는 이로, 7세 경에 하나씩 빠져 영구치가 나온다.

I wasn't too **thrill**ed about that. But my dad said we'd go for chocolate milkshakes **afterward**. So that was something. My mom and dad are **divorce**d, by the way. I spend half the time with each of them. My dad is a writer, and he works at home. So he's the one who takes me to **stuff** like orthodontists and milkshakes.

Dad and I were sitting in the waiting room. My old orthodontist, Dr. Silver, had **retire**d. Now there was a new guy named Dr. Sheldon Jekyll. I knew because he sent me a card with a **smiley** face[4] on it. It was the first smiley face I'd seen with teeth in it. Very straight teeth.

---

4 smiley face 사람의 웃는 얼굴을 나타내기 위해 노란색 원 안에 검은색으로 두 눈과 웃는 입 모양을 그려 넣은 단순한 그림.

When I first heard Dr. Jekyll's name, I got a little **spook**ed. There's this really scary book called *Dr. Jekyll and Mr. Hyde*.[5] It's by Steven Louis Robertson. Or maybe it's Robert Louis Stevenson.[6] Anyway, it's somebody like that. Maybe you've read it. It's about this nice doctor who **turn**s **into** a **monster** named Edward Hyde. It happens every time he drinks some kind of **potion**.

I **joke**d with my dad about it. He said it was just a **made-up** story. And things like that don't happen in real life. He always says stuff like that. But I know better.

---

5 **Dr. Jekyll and Mr. Hyde** 영국의 소설가 로버트 루이스 스티븐슨이 1886년에 발표한 소설인 《지킬 박사와 하이드 씨》. 선한 성격의 지킬 박사가 특수한 약물을 마시고 사악한 인격의 하이드로 변한다는 이야기이다.

6 **Robert Louis Stevenson** 로버트 루이스 스티븐슨.《보물섬》,《지킬 박사와 하이드 씨》 등으로 유명한 영국의 소설가이자 시인. 주로 교훈이 담긴 모험담과 환상적인 세계에 대한 이야기를 썼다.

While Dad and I were sitting in the waiting room I **notice**d this much older girl. She was about thirteen. I'm ten. She smiled at me. Boy,⁷ were her teeth straight! They **remind**ed me of Dr. Jekyll's smiley face card. I guess going to an orthodontist was really working for her.

Just then the nurse told me to go in.

"Do you want me to go in with you?" asked my dad.

"Uh, no," I said. "Why?"

"Well, **in case** you were **scare**d about having your tooth out. Or because you haven't met Dr. Jekyll before."

"Oh," I said. I did sort of want Dad to

---

7 **boy** 여기에서는 '소년'이라는 뜻이 아니라, '맙소사!' 또는 '어머나!'라는 의미로 놀람이나 기쁨 등을 나타내는 표현으로 쓰였다.

come in with me. But I didn't want to look like a big baby in front of that girl. "I think I'd like to go in alone, Dad," I said.

"OK," said Dad. He gave me a **squeeze**.

I went in to meet Dr. Jekyll.

Well, Dr. Jekyll wasn't at all scary looking. He had black hair **comb**ed straight back. He seemed really **jolly**. And he had a big smile. I mean we're talking **wall-to-wall** teeth.

"Hello!" he said. "Glad to meet you, Zack. Glad to meet you. I'm sure we'll **get along** just fine. And I promise not to pull the wrong tooth. Ha, ha. That was a little joke."

I smiled weakly. Then we shook hands. His hand was **sweaty**. He seemed a little

fidgety. Well, I was a little fidgety myself. But I was the one having the tooth pulled. I don't know what *his* **excuse** was.

"Well, well, sit down, Zack. Sit down," said Dr. Jekyll. He **rub**bed his hands together. Like he was **eager** to get to work.

"Right in that chair there. That's right. Let me look at that tooth now. Open wide. Open wider. Aha! Yes. I see the little **devil**. Ha, ha. We can't have you making Zack's **grown-up** tooth[8] grow in **crook**ed, now, can we? We're going to have to **yank** you out of there, you little devil, aren't we? Ha, ha."

OK. Calling my tooth a little devil was

---

8 **grown-up tooth** 영구치(permanent tooth). 'adult tooth'라고도 한다. 젖니가 빠진 뒤에 나오는 이로 죽을 때까지 평생 사용한다.

a **tiny** bit weird. Talking to a tooth *at all* was weird. I **admit** that. But **otherwise**, I thought he seemed pretty normal.

"Zack," said Dr. Jekyll, rubbing his hands some more, "I'm going to give you nitrous oxide.[9] Do you know what that is?"

"Laughing gas?" I said.

"**Exact**ly," he said. "Have you ever had nitrous oxide before?"

"No, sir," I said.

"Well, I think you'll like it," he said.

He placed a mask over my nose. A long **tube** connected it to a **tank** of gas on the floor. He **turn**ed it **on**. I heard a **hiss**ing

---

9 **nitrous oxide** 아산화 질소. 무색 투명한 기체로 마취 및 진통 효과가 있어 수술이나 치과 치료 등에서 마취제로 사용한다. 흡입시 웃는 것처럼 보이거나 심하게 웃게 해서 '웃음 가스(laughing gas)'라고 부르기도 한다.

sound.

At first I didn't feel anything. Then I began to get **dizzy**. And then my head seemed to get very light. Just like a helium[10] balloon. I felt if I didn't **hold on to** it, my head would **float** right up to the **ceiling**.

I could see it. My head *was* a helium balloon. Floating on the ceiling. Suddenly that seemed the funniest thing I had ever thought of. I started to **giggle**. Dr. Jekyll giggled, too. I laughed **hysterica**lly. So did Dr. Jekyll.

Then he took a pair of **plier**s and pulled my tooth. I thought *that* was funny, too.

---

10 helium 헬륨. 공기 중에 아주 적은 양만 들어 있는 무색무취의 기체. 공기보다 가볍기 때문에 풍선이나 비행선 등을 공중에 띄우는 데 사용한다.

Dr. Jekyll must have thought it was even funnier than I did. He was laughing so hard, his face got red. Then it got purple. Then his eyes sort of **bulge**d out and got wild looking.

I thought he might be having a heart attack.[11] And for some reason I thought that was funny, too. He started **stagger**ing around the office. He looked like one of the Three Stooges.[12] I was laughing so hard I was almost **choking**.

Then—and I'm not sure about this— it seemed his hair grew longer. And

---

11 **heart attack** 심장 마비. 심장의 기능이 갑자기 멈추는 일. 주로 심장 내 혈액의 흐름이 원활하지 않을 때 발생한다.

12 **Three Stooges** 쓰리 스투지스. '세 명의 멍청이'라는 뜻으로, 1920년대 부터 70년대까지 미국에서 큰 인기를 누린 공연이자 3인조 코미디 팀이다. 과장된 몸짓과 치고받는 동작으로 이루어진 코미디로 유명하다.

his teeth were growing, too. Long and crooked. Like **fang**s. I was laughing so hard, I was **gasp**ing.

Dr. Jekyll wasn't laughing anymore. He was **growl**ing.

"Oh, no!" he shouted. "It's happening again! I can't believe it! I can't stop it! Aaarrrgghh! AAARRRGGHH!"

Chapter 2

Dr. Jekyll kept **stagger**ing all over the office. His hair was wild and crazy looking. He started toward me, the **plier**s still in his hand. It looked like he was getting ready to pull another tooth. Oh, no!

"Help!" I shouted. "Get me out of here!"

But I was still laughing. It was the

weirdest feeling I've ever had. Being **scare**d to death and being unable to stop laughing.

Dr. Jekyll came closer. I couldn't move my arms or legs. It felt like I was **strap**ped into the chair.

All of a sudden Dr. Jekyll **lurch**ed to a stop.

"What am I doing?" he cried. "I must stop this."

He **grab**bed a bottle off a **shelf**. He **tore** off the top. He **gulp**ed it down.

A second later Dr. Jekyll stopped **growl**ing. He stopped staggering around. His hair lay back down on his head. His teeth grew back into his mouth. His face went from purple to red. Then from

red to pink. He **clear**ed **his throat**. He **pat**ted his hair. He looked **nervous**ly at me and smiled. Nice straight TV-**ad** teeth again.

He **took** the gas mask **off** my face.

"Well, now," he said. "How do we feel?"

"Uh, I can only speak for myself," I said.

"And how do *you* feel?"

"OK, I guess," I said.

I was telling a **huge fib**. I didn't really feel OK at all. I just said that **in case** Dr. Jekyll was getting ready to go **berserk** on me again. I was pretty **shaken** up, if you want to know the truth. My old orthodontist, Dr. Silver, **hardly** ever went berserk on me.

Dr. Jekyll was putting a **wad** of **cotton** into my mouth. Then he put the pulled tooth in a **tiny** blue plastic box that **was supposed to** look like a **treasure chest**.

"That little **devil** is right in here now, where he **belong**s," said Dr. Jekyll. He handed me the little plastic treasure chest.

The laughing gas had **worn off** by now. I started to wonder. Had I really seen what I thought I saw? Or was it just some kind of crazy dream? Maybe it was something the laughing gas did to me. But it had all seemed so real.

Dr. Jekyll handed me a little paper cup. "What's this?" I asked.

"It's just **mouthwash**," he said. "Miracle Mouthwash. It's truly **yummy**. I **invent**ed it. Try it."

I tried it. It did **taste** pretty good. Sort of like bubble **gum**. And a little bit like peanut butter and chocolate. I **swish**ed some around in my mouth. I **spit** it out in the spit **bowl**.

"Don't spit!" shouted Dr. Jekyll. "DON'T SPIT!"

Uh-oh, I thought. Here we go again.

Then, in a much **calm**er voice, he said, "This is *special* mouthwash, Zack. It's all right to drink it."

"Really?" I said. I took another cup and **swallow**ed it down. "No **dentist** has ever told me I could drink mouthwash before."

"Well, Zack, I'm not like other dentists," he said.

Boy, you can say *that* again,[1] I thought.

---

1 **you can say that again** 다른 사람이 하는 말에 동의할 때 사용하는 표현으로 '정말 그렇다!' 또는 '동감이야!'라는 뜻이다.

Chapter 3

I waited till we were out of the office and in the coffee shop before I told Dad what happened. I looked around to make sure nobody could hear me.

"Dad, what would you say if I told you that when I was in Dr. Jekyll's office he **turn**ed **into** a **monster**?"

Dad **chuckle**d.

"I'd say you had a great **imagination**," he said.

Dad was having a chocolate milkshake, too. Part of it was on his upper **lip**, like a **mustache**.

"Yeah, but that's what really happened," I said. "I think."

"What are you talking about?"

A man and woman sat down in a **booth** behind me. I **lean**ed in close to Dad and **whisper**ed.

"Dad," I said, "right after Dr. Jekyll pulled my tooth, he started changing. His face turned purple. His hair grew wild. His teeth grew long and **crook**ed. He started **growl**ing. And he said something about how it was happening again, and how he couldn't stop it."

Dad looked at me to see if I was **put**ting him **on**. I wasn't.

"And then what?" he asked.

"And then he drank some **stuff** out of a bottle. And he **calm**ed right down again," I said.

Dad was looking at me strangely. I **slurp**ed up some of my milkshake. It **taste**d really good. Even better than Dr. Jekyll's **mouthwash**.

"And this happened when?" Dad asked.

"Well . . . let's see. He gave me the laughing gas and . . ." I went no further.

Dad was **nod**ding and smiling. He seemed **relieve**d. He **wipe**d his mouth with a **napkin**. No more mustache.

"You've never had nitrous oxide before, have you?" he said.

"No, but . . ."

"I think it was just the gas," he said. "First time **and all**."

Well, it was certainly possible.

"Maybe you're right," I said.

"I **doubt** you'll ever experience anything like that again," he said. "As long as you live."

Dad had no idea how wrong he was.

Chapter 4

When I woke up the next morning my mouth hurt where my tooth was pulled. I went into the bathroom. I pulled my **lip** way down and **peer**ed into the mirror. The hole looked fine. But the teeth next to it looked **funny**. I thought they looked more crooked. But how could that be? Probably it was my **imagination**.

I didn't think about it until a few days later. I was watching TV and laughing pretty hard. Dad looked at me strangely.

"What is it?" I asked.

"Have you been wearing your **retainer** at night?" he asked.

"Sure," I said.

"Even when you're at Mom's apartment?"

"Of course," I said. "Why?"

"It just seemed to me your teeth were looking a little crooked," he said. "It's probably just my imagination."

"No, Dad," I said. "I think they're more crooked, too."

My teeth *felt* more crooked. The two big front ones **most of all**.

Two days later I was back at Dr. Jekyll's

office for my **follow-up** visit. I was going to ask him about my teeth. Dad left me in the waiting room. He had some things to do. He said he'd be back in half an hour.

The same girl I saw before was there. She was on her way out. She smiled at me again. Funny. Her teeth looked more crooked than they did the last time.

What was going on here?

The nurse went down the **hall** to Dr. Jekyll's office to help him with a **patient**. I was all alone in the waiting room.

I **notice**d the nurse had left the file **cabinet** open. It had all the kids' files in it. I knew that in my file there was this photo of me. It was taken before I got my retainer. My teeth were real crooked then.

I was **scare**d they were getting that way again.

I knew the files were **private**. But I really wanted to see that photo of me. Before I could stop myself, I walked over to the cabinet. I started **look**ing **through** the **folder**s.

I couldn't find mine. But I found something else. It was a file **mark**ed "Dr. Jekyll—**Personal**." I know what I did next was wrong. But I **peek**ed inside. There was a big **envelope**. Inside was a diary. I read one of the pages.

"Day 13. The **experiment**s continue to go well. But they must remain secret for now. No one has ever done this before."

Secret experiments! Yes! Dr. Jekyll **was**

up to no good.

Just then I heard **footstep**s. Was the nurse coming back? I **panic**ked. I closed the **drawer**. I went and **slip**ped the diary into my **book bag**. Then I remembered the nurse had left the cabinet open. I **race**d back and opened it again.

The nurse came back into the waiting room. She looked at me.

"What are you doing in my file cabinet?" she said.

Chapter 5

The nurse looked angry.

"Those files are **private**," she said.

"It's OK," I said. "I didn't see anything."

"What didn't you see?" she asked.

"Anything," I said. "Any diaries or anything else."

Probably that wasn't the smartest thing to say. But it was all I could think of.

Luckily the phone **rang** just then. The nurse **pick**ed it **up**. The voice on the other end of the **line** was so loud I could almost **make out** the words. The voice sounded really angry.

"No, no, Mrs. Fortensky," said the nurse. "Surely Whitney's teeth can't be getting *more* **crook**ed."

There was more **yell**ing from the angry voice.

"Yes, Mrs. Fortensky, I'm sure you have very good eyes," said the nurse.

There was more yelling.

"Of course the doctor can see Whitney this afternoon," said the nurse. "Come in at four o'clock."

So! Other kids were getting crooked

teeth, too! I had to read that diary. Then I'd know what Dr. Jekyll **was up to**. But right now Dr. Jekyll was calling me into his office.

"So," said Dr. Jekyll. "How are you today, Zack?"

He was smiling like he had just eaten a **canary**[1] or something.

"OK," I said.

"Any problems?"

He was **rub**bing his hands together like they were cold. He looked kind of **antsy**, too. Just like the last time.

He had me sit down in the **dentist**'s chair.

---

1 **like he had just eaten a canary** 숙어 'like the cat that ate the canary'에서 나온 표현으로 '의기양양한' 또는 '우쭐해하는'이라는 뜻이다.

"Nope," I said. "No problems, sir."

"Good," he said. "How did that **gum heal** where I pulled the tooth?"

"Fine," I said.

"Excellent," he said.

He looked inside my mouth.

"Your mouth looks great, Zack," he said.

"It does?" I said.

"Really, really great."

"You don't think my teeth are just a little more crooked than last time?"

"Oh, no," he said. "That can't be. **Absolutely** not. In fact, I think they're getting straighter. They *have* to be getting straighter. Much straighter. Why do you ask?"

"No reason," I said. I thought I'd better

drop it. Dr. Jekyll was starting to get **work**ed **up**.

Right after he was done **examining** me, he gave me a little paper cup.

"What's this?" I asked. "More Miracle **Mouthwash**?"

"That's right, Zack," he said in this kind of **fake** television-**announcer** voice. "Miracle Mouthwash. It's delicious and **nutritious**. And it builds strong teeth in twelve ways."

I took a **sip**. I **swish**ed it around in my mouth.

"Drink it up," he said in the same **eager** voice. "It's good—and so good *for* you."

I **pretend**ed to **swallow**.

"There now," he said. "Isn't that yum-dilly-icious?[2]"

I **nod**ded.

"Well, **so long**, Zack," said Dr. Jekyll,
shaking my hand. "Come and see me
again in a month."

I didn't say anything. I couldn't. My
cheeks were full of mouthwash.

---

2 **yum-dilly-icious** 주로 아이들이 사용하는 'yum-delicious(냠냠 맛있
다)'라는 말에 'deli-' 대신 'dilly(놀라운)'를 넣어 정말 맛있다는 것을 강
조한 표현.

Chapter 6

Dad was in the waiting room. The second we got outside, I **spit** the mouthwash out on the **sidewalk**.

"What was that?" Dad asked.

"Miracle Mouthwash," I said.

Dad looked at me and **frown**ed.

"Dr. Jekyll wanted me to drink it," I explained. "I didn't think I should."

"I've never heard of a dentist telling a **patient** to drink mouthwash," Dad said.

"Neither have I," I said. "That's why I decided not to."

I started to tell Dad about the diary. Then I stopped. Dad was going to be mad. Better if he got mad at home. So I waited till we were back at the apartment. I wasn't sure how to start.

"Dad," I said, "when I was in the waiting room, I **look**ed **through** Dr. Jekyll's file **cabinet**."

"What?" he said.

"I'm sure my teeth are getting more crooked," I **went on**. "So I wanted to find that photo of me before I started wearing my **retainer**. Just to check. Instead I found

something else . . . Dr. Jekyll's diary. And
. . . I took it."

"You *took* it?" he said. Dad **sank** down in
his chair. "I can't believe you did that!"

He looked really **upset**.

"Dad," I said, "I can't believe I did it
either. But I *have* to read this diary. I'm sure
it will **prove** to you that Dr. Jekyll is **weird**.
And **up to no good**."

I took the diary out of my **book bag**. I
opened it and began to read:

"'The **experiment**s continue to go well.
The **subject**s seem to like the **taste**. I like it,
too. In fact, I love it. I mean, I really love it.
It's yum-dilly-icious.'"

"Yum-dilly-icious?" said my dad.

"He used that same word in the office

today."

"Well, it's a pretty **goofy** word," said my dad. "But it doesn't make him a **criminal**. And it's no reason to **swipe** the man's diary."

That was true. Still, I was pretty sure Dr. Jekyll was doing weird **stuff**.

"Let me keep reading," I said. "'. . . My Miracle Mouthwash will be every bit as wonderful as I **suspect**ed. Just think of it— a way to **straighten** teeth without **brace**s! When the world hears about this, I shall become famous. Perhaps someone will even give me my own TV talk show.'"

"A way to straighten teeth without braces?" said my dad. "What a great idea!"

True again. But something was

wrong. I had drunk some of his Miracle Mouthwash. And it sure wasn't making my teeth straighter.

"Let me read more," I said. "'. . . To be **absolutely** safe, I have developed Anti-[1] Miracle Mouthwash. It can **immediate**ly **reverse** any **side effect**s. **In case** anything ever goes wrong. Which it never will. But still.'"

"Dr. Jekyll wants to **guard** against side effects," said my dad. "That sounds pretty **responsible**."

"Dad!" I said. "Whose **side** are you on here? OK, listen to this: 'Saw seventeen patients today. All had at least one **dose**

---

1 **anti-** 형용사나 명사와 함께 쓰이는 접두사로 '~을 방지하는'이라는 뜻 이다.

of Miracle Mouthwash. Many **complain**ed their teeth were *more* crooked. But I know that can't be so. **After all**, my subjects in the back room are **respond**ing so well! My Miracle Mouthwash is **transform**ing them just as I planned. And they no longer seem to **mind** being kept here.'"

I looked up at Dad in **horror**.

"Dad, *he's keeping people in the back room! Against their will!*"

"It doesn't say against their will," said Dad. But he didn't sound so sure anymore. "It just says they're being kept in the back room. There must be some perfectly good explanation."

"Like what?"

"I don't know," he said. "Maybe they're

out-of-towners. And they can't **afford** a hotel. And he's doing them a **favor** by letting them stay there."

"I don't think so," I said. Then I read some more. "Take a look at this: 'I find I am loving the mouthwash more and more. I cannot seem to get enough of it. I just had some a minute ago, and already I . . . Oh, no! It's happening ag . . .'" I showed Dad the diary. "See. The writing gets all **wobbly** here. And then it just kind of **dribble**s off the page."

Dad took a close look.

"Zack," he said, "I **admit** this is a little strange."

"Yes! And I **bet** Dr. Jekyll was looking a little strange, too. Right after he wrote that."

I could just **picture** it. The **fang**s. The wild hair. The **buggy** eyes.

"Don't you get it?" I said. "Dr. Jekyll must have started **turn**ing **into** a **monster** again. Dad, I want to go back to his office tonight. After everybody has gone home."

"And do what?" he asked.

"See what's in that back room."

Dad **thought** this **over**. He shook his head.

"The only reason I'd go there tonight," he said, "would be to put that diary back before anybody knows you swiped it. I don't like what you did. Not at all."

I **broke out** in a big **grin**.

"You mean you'll actually go with me?"

I said.

"Only to put back that diary," he said.

Chapter 7

After dinner, Dad and I went back to Dr. Jekyll's office building. A **guard** asked us to **sign** his book. We had to **print** our names and the time we entered. Dad **put down** "Edward Hyde and son." Ha, ha! Then we went up in the elevator.

We were lucky. The cleaning people were just leaving Dr. Jekyll's office.

"Hold the door," said my dad. And they did.

"I'm Dr. Jekyll," said Dad. "I forgot something in my office."

Wow! Dad was getting good at this **break**ing**-and-enter**ing stuff!

As soon as the cleaning people were gone, I went right to the file **cabinet**. I opened the **drawer** and put back the diary.

"Now let's go," said my dad.

"No," I said. "First we have to see who's in that back room. If I don't, I'll never know for sure what's going on."

Dad looked at me hard. He had a **frown** on his face. Then he **shrug**ged and **nod**ded.

We went down the **hall** past the **examining** rooms. We turned left. And there it was. A door with a sign on it: BACK ROOM. We pushed it open.

Inside it was **complete**ly dark. From somewhere we could hear the soft **trickle** of running water.

I tried to find a light **switch**, but couldn't. In the dark we could hear something else. The sound of living things.

At last I found the switch.

I **turn**ed **on** the lights.

Dad and I both **gasp**ed.

There were the **subject**s of Dr. Jekyll's **experiment**s.

And . . . they weren't human!

Chapter 8

$\mathcal{S}$everal pairs of large yellow eyes **stare**d back at us. Their faces were **cover**ed with brown hair.

"Oh, no," said Dad softly. "They're . . ."

". . . beavers,[1]" I said.

Yes, beavers. Three groups of beavers.

---

1 **beaver** 비버. 꼬리가 편평하며 비늘로 덮여 있고 뒷발에 물갈퀴가 발달해 있어 수중생활에 적응되어 있다. 댐을 만드는 것으로 유명하다.

Each group had built a beaver **lodge** in a **pool** of water with small trees around it.

"Very strange," said Dad.

I looked at him and smiled this big smile.

"I told you so," I said.

"Strange, but also not against the **law**," said Dad.

We closed the door behind us. We walked closer to the beavers. The first beaver lodge had a little **sign** on it: **CONTROL** GROUP.[2] NO MIRACLE MOUTHWASH. The beavers in this group looked like normal beavers. With big **buck teeth**. They were swimming around

---

2 **control group** 통제 집단. 실험 연구에서 실험의 효과를 비교하기 위해 선정된 집단으로, 아무런 처리나 치료를 하지 않는다.

in their **tank**. Putting finishing **touch**es
on their lodge. Busy as . . . OK, busy as
beavers.[3]

Their lodge looked like a normal beaver
lodge. It was nicely built, with good **sturdy**
branches. The ends were **chew**ed off
cleanly.

The sign on the second lodge said: TEST
GROUP[4] 1. MOUTHWASH FOR 3 WEEKS. The
beavers in this group had much straighter
teeth. They were swimming around, trying
to build their lodge. But they were having
trouble **gnaw**ing the branches.

---

3 **busy as beavers** '몹시 바쁜'이라는 뜻의 숙어. 유사한 표현으로 'busy as a bee'가 있다.

4 **test group** 실험 집단. 실험 연구에서 실험의 효과를 확인하기 위해 어떤 처리나 치료를 실제로 받는 집단. 통제 집단과 차이점을 비교하여 효과를 확인한다.

Their lodge didn't look so hot. The ends of the branches were sort of **shred**ded. The **roof** looked like it was ready to **cave in**.

The sign on the third lodge said: TEST GROUP 2. MOUTHWASH FOR 5 WEEKS. The beavers in this group had great teeth. But their lodge was **pathetic**. No **self-respecting** beaver would ever want to live in it.

One of the beavers with straight teeth swam over and gave me a smile. His teeth were perfect. But I felt sorry for him.

"Dad," I said. "Beavers **were** never **meant to** have straight teeth. It goes against all the laws of nature."

"Perhaps you're right," he said.

"I don't get it," I said. "I thought

Miracle Mouthwash made teeth **crook**ed. But with these beavers . . ."

I **frown**ed. I **scratch**ed my head. And then it **hit** me!

"Dad!" I said. "I think I understand! The mouthwash works on animals, but not on people! That's why my teeth are getting crooked! And that girl in the waiting room—" I **shudder**ed. "Who even *knows* what she looks like now!"

On a **shelf** at the end of the room was a **row** of bottles. I went and took a closer look at them. One bottle was **label**ed Anti-Miracle Mouthwash.

"Look," I said. "I think this is the **stuff** that Dr. Jekyll drank after he **turn**ed **into** a **monster**. Remember the diary? I think this is what turns him back into his normal self."

"What if we **fed** it to the beavers?" Dad asked. "Do you think it might make their teeth turn back into normal beaver teeth again?"

"It's sure **worth** a try," I said.

Just then there was a **terrible** noise in the outer office. Things were **crash**ing to the floor. Glass was breaking. Something large was **bump**ing into walls. It sounded like there was an **ape loose**.

Before we could hide, the door to the back room **burst** open. It hit Dad in the head. Dad **sank** to the floor.

He was **out cold**!

And in the **doorway** stood Dr. Jekyll.

Dr. Jekyll's hair was standing straight out. His eyes were **bulging** and **bloodshot** . . . and he was looking straight at me!

Chapter 9

"MOUTHWASH!" shouted Dr. Jekyll. "NEED MIRACLE MOUTHWASH! NONE AT HOME! NONE HERE! NEED MORE! NEED MORE NOW! AAARRRGGHH!"

"Hi there, Dr. Jekyll," I said, trying to sound normal. "And how are you this evening, sir?"

"MIRACLE MOUTHWASH!" **roar**ed

Jekyll. "CAN'T FIND ANY! NEED IT! NEED IT NOW! AAARRRGGHH!"

"Dr. Jekyll," I said. "I know you mean well, but your mouthwash isn't working. Look at me. Look at you! I don't want to be **mean**, but you're a **mess**. Miracle Mouthwash may **straighten** teeth on beavers. But it does the **opposite** to humans. The thing is—"

"MOUTHWASH! NOW! NOW!"

It was no use trying to talk to Dr. Jekyll. He was running around the room like a **madman**. But I had a plan. I **grab**bed the bottle of Anti-Miracle Mouthwash. I **slip**ped it into my pocket.

"Yoo hoo, Dr. Jekyll!" I called. "I know where we can find some mouthwash!"

"WHERE? WHERE MOUTHWASH? GIVE ME MOUTHWASH!"

"Follow me, sir," I said with a smile. I led the way down the **hall**.

"MOUTHWASH?"

"Right this way, sir," I said.

Dr. Jekyll followed me into his office.

"WHERE MOUTHWASH? HERE? NOT HERE! ALREADY LOOKED HERE!"

"I have it," I said. "Sit right down in this **dentist**'s chair, sir. Just **relax**. And I'll give it to you."

Jekyll sat down in his dentist's chair. The moment he did, I grabbed the mask with the laughing gas. I **clamp**ed it down over his nose. I **turn**ed **on** the gas.

Right away the gas started **hiss**ing. And

Dr. Jekyll started **giggling**.

"Good boy," I said. "Very good boy! And as soon as we're done, you can go to the toy **bin** and choose a little plastic **dinosaur** to take home with you."

I **took** the mask **off** Dr. Jekyll's face. He was laughing like a madman. I took out the bottle of Anti-Miracle Mouthwash.

"Now open wide," I said in my best dentist-sounding voice. "Open wider. A little wider. Good boy!"

Before he could see what it was, I **pour**ed the whole bottle down Dr. Jekyll's **throat**.

Gulp! Down it went.

Dr. Jekyll kept laughing. He **struggle**d for a few moments. Then he stopped.

Little by little, Dr. Jekyll returned to normal. He stopped **foam**ing at the mouth. His hair grew shorter and **neat**er. His eyes stopped **bulging** out. His crazy teeth got smaller.

"Whew!" he said. "Where am I? What happened?" Then he looked at me. And it seemed to **come back** to him. "Heh, heh, this is a little **embarrass**ing," he said.

"Embarrassing?" I said. "It's **horrible**! What you did to those poor beavers! Beavers who never did you any **harm**! Beavers **are supposed to** have **buck teeth**, not straight ones."

"But it's **for the greater good**," said Dr. Jekyll. "I'm going to straighten children's teeth without **brace**s. With my Miracle

Mouthwash."

"But it's not working on people!" I said. "Can't you **get** that **through your head**? Look at me! I'm starting to look like Bugs Bunny![1]"

Dr. Jekyll looked at me. Then he put his head in his hands.

"I never **intend**ed to hurt either kids or beavers," he said.

"Well, you have," I said.

"I guess man **was** not **meant to tamper** with the unknown," said Dr. Jekyll. "Man was not meant to drink mouthwash."

He looked up at me from the dentist's

---

1 **Bugs Bunny** 벅스 버니. 미국 워너브라더스(Warner Brothers) 제작사에서 회색 토끼를 의인화해서 만든 애니메이션 캐릭터. 튀어나온 앞니와 짓궂고 능글맞은 성격이 특징이다.

chair.

"Zack, I **owe** you a great **deal**," he said. "What can I do to **repay** you?"

"Give Anti-Miracle Mouthwash to all the kids," I said. "And give it to all the beavers. Promise never to drink Miracle Mouthwash again. **Destroy** any you have left."

"I promise," said Dr. Jekyll.

Just then Dad **stagger**ed in from the back room. He had a **bump** the size of an egg on his **forehead**.

"Dad, **thank heavens** you're OK!" I said.

"What happened?" Dad asked.

"Well," I said, "my **patient** here was having some problems. But we **clear**ed them all **up**, didn't we?"

I looked at Dr. Jekyll. He **nod**ded.

Once he was back to normal, Dr. Jekyll was **as good as his word**. He gave Anti-Miracle Mouthwash to all the kids whose teeth had gotten **crook**ed. Mine got straight again right away. So did the girl's in the waiting room.

The beavers were fine, too. The ones with straight teeth got big buck ones again. Dr. Jekyll **donate**d all the beavers to the Bronx Zoo.[2] I visit them there whenever I can. Their beaver **lodge**s are so nice now, they could be in a magazine.

Because he was so **grateful**, Dr. Jekyll

---

2 **Bronx Zoo** 브롱크스 동물원. 미국 뉴욕주(州) 브롱크스(Bronx) 지구에 있으며, 뉴욕 동물원이라고도 부른다. 미국에서 가장 큰 동물원이다.

also promised me free **dental** work for the rest of my life. Dad was really glad about that.

And since then I never, never drink mouthwash at the dentist's office.

I don't think you should, either.